My-Twenty-One

Shivechha Panghal

BookLeaf Publishing

Presentation by *BookLeaf Publishing*

Web: www.bookleafpub.com

E-mail: info@bookleafpub.com

ISBN: 9789357748698

First edition 2023

This book is dedicated to everyone who knows
the number Twenty-one exists!!

ACKNOWLEDGEMENT

Hello reader,
My deepest appreciation goes to my family and friends who have been my pillars of strength and support throughout my journey. Your unwavering support, encouragement, and love have been my constant motivation to pursue my passion for writing. And of course, my teachers played their roles in their own special way.
I also extend my appreciation to the random people I have met throughout my life, who somehow left an indelible mark and taught me something new. Your brief encounters and life lessons inspired some of the poems in this book, for which I am grateful.
So this book of poems is dedicated to all those who have touched my life in various ways. Your positive impact has been immeasurable and has fueled my creativity and imagination.

With gratitude,
Shivechha

PREFACE

To my reader,

It is with great pleasure that I share with you my collection of 21 poems, each one unique in its own way.

I chose to write about a variety of topics, my hope is that readers will find something in each of these poems that speaks to them on a personal level, and that they will be able to take away something meaningful from each and every one.

Through my writing, I aim to help my readers muse themselves, to gain a new perspective on life, and to learn something new as they spend their precious time reading these 21 poems. My unique style of writing is intended to grab the reader's attention and create an emotional connection with each poem.

Twenty-one is a number that is dear to me, and by the end of this book, I hope that the number 21 becomes dear to you as well.

Thank you for choosing to embark on this journey with me, and I hope that my poems will leave a positive and lasting impact on your life.

Genuinely & honestly,
Shivechha

Next time the world seems cruel, know that you are Hope

Surrounded by towering trees so grand,
A small bud lies on the forest floor,
Where sunlight can barely reach its hand,
And shadows swirl around it more.

It feels like it's fighting a losing game,
That the odds are stacked against its growth,
That life is always going to be the same,
With obstacles that it cannot clothe.

But as the seasons come and go,
The small bud learns to find its way,
To stand up tall and let its beauty show,
And grow stronger with each passing day.

Its roots run deep and its stem grows strong,
And though the forest still looms ahead,
The small plant knows that it belongs,
And no longer feels so filled with dread.

For life may present us with towering trees,
And shadows that seem too hard to bear,
But if we believe in ourselves and seize,
Our inner strength we can declare.

So take heart, dear friend, and let your spirit soar,
Like that small bud in the midst of the forest floor,
For with patience, perseverance, and a hopeful heart,
You too can overcome and make a beautiful start.

Whatever done without Faith is useless

In life, so much is done in vain,
Without faith, our efforts are inane.
Aloe vera on our faces, we try at home,
My brother questions the process, with a
doubtful tone.

But I put it on with faith, hopeful and sure,
Believing it will work, my skin will lure.
Faith is the catalyst that sets us apart,
It gives us the courage to follow our heart.

Without it, we'd falter and fall,
But with faith, we rise above it all.
It helps us win battles, so tough and grim,
Throughout history, its power has been seen
within.

Positivity and optimism, it adds to our stride,
With faith, there's no stopping, nowhere to hide.
It's an unmatchable asset, to our personality,
With faith's great power, we can achieve all we
can see.

So, next time you attempt something new,
Do it with faith, and see it through.
The fruits of your labor will be sweet and true,
Believing in yourself, all your dreams will come
through.

If you lost a loved one, know that I feel you

The pain is deep and hard to bear,
For those who've lost a loved one dear,
The emptiness is all you feel,
A void that time can never heal.

You cry and cry, but tears won't cease,
The thought of life without them is not a breeze,
It's too big to process, too hard to accept,
You long for them, every moment kept.

Years pass by, but agony lingers on,
The sorrow deepens, as time moves on,
Every photo, every memory,
Reminds you of what you've lost, you see.

You pray for them to come back, but in vain,
The reality is hard, it's not the same,
You're not ready to believe they're gone,
You cling to hope, your love lives on.

But in your heart, there's a glimmer of truth,
That maybe God loved them more in their youth,
And they're happy where they are,
With loved ones who've gone far.

They might be planning to take birth again,
And meet you in some other plane,
This life is just a small part,
Of the journey of your beating heart.

So hold on tight, and keep yourself warm,
For no one else will, during this storm,
Things will fall into place, one day,
And you'll smile with the memories, and find
your way.

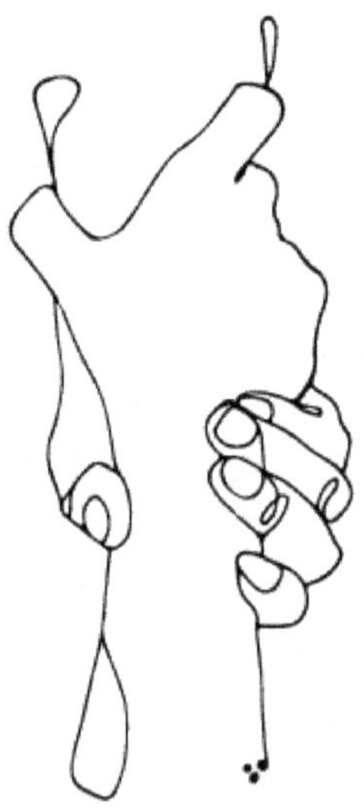

Tell her that she is a LOTUS

My dear woman, you are a Lotus,
A symbol of strength and pureness,
You rise from the mud without stain,
And shine bright, like the sun after rain.

You are as sacred as worshiping can be,
And auspicious, just like the Lotus tree,
You stand out like a distinct flower,
And have the power to move mountains higher.

You're a badass draped in a saree,
And can achieve what most can never dream or
see,
From fighting household battles to serving the
nation,
You're always striving for human progression.

You're a Lotus, and always will be,
A symbol of purity and rebirth, you'll never
cease to see,
You can rise and bloom above the mud,
And inspire others to stand up, and rise above.

So let's be proud of being a Lotus,
And keep blooming without fear or fuss,
For we are strong, and never will fall,
And to the world, we'll always stand tall.

You are a LOTUS.

Next time you lose a balloon
to the sky, smile

Up, up, up it goes,
A balloon, to everyone's woes.
No place to go, but up,
Leave your troubles in your cup.

Life is like a balloon,
Don't hold back, take it to the moon.
The fun stuff is up high,
Spread your wings, just try.

The balloon, a symbol of hope,
A smile to those who cannot cope.
Peace in a world of chaos,
A message to all those at a loss.

May it bring grins by the dozen,
Lift us all up, above the buzzin'.
May we practice virtues every day,
And say goodbye to any dismay.

One balloon away from a good mood,
Oh yes, this feeling is simply too good.
Go buy a balloon, make it fly,
And remember, to the sky it's okay to say goodbye.

Anger is your best friend

Anger, a fiery emotion we all know,
It can burn and scorch, but there's more to show.
It's beautiful, in a different kind of way,
It teaches us about our trigger points, every day.

The things we can't settle with, it highlights,
And gently nudges us towards what we need to
fight.
It's an emergency light, to abort from a spot,
Which doesn't belong to us, anger helps us a lot.

It's often seen as negative, but let us look
beyond,
Anger's just an emotion, not a venom or a bond.
It's seemingly negative, with positive effects
galore,
More positive than the positive emotions we
adore.

If we change our perspective, we can learn a lot,
About our personality and behaviour, and what
we've got.
It can teach us to recognize, what we don't want
in our lives,
And prioritize the things we want, without any
lies.

So, let's embrace anger, in a positive way,
It teaches us and helps us grow, every single day.
Let's learn our lessons well, and use them to our
advantage,
To conquer our fears, and boldly turn the page.

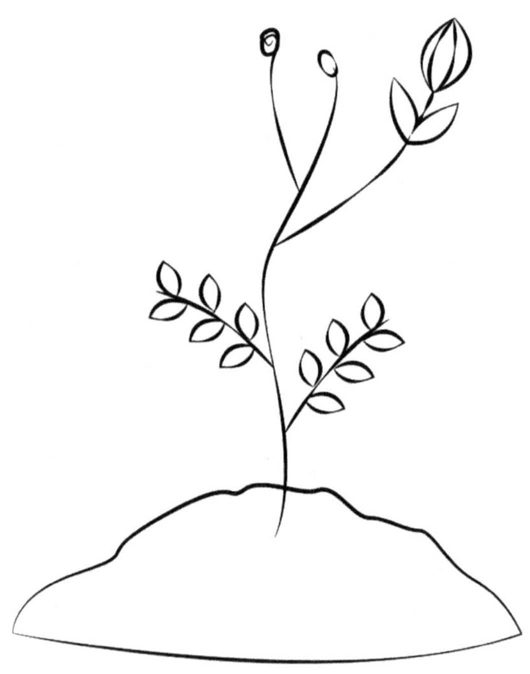

Depression, I know how it feels, I am proud of you for thriving it alone

Everything around me seems so dark,
My heart feels heavy, like it's lost its spark.
I have no appetite, my favorite food,
No longer tastes good.

Things that used to make me happy,
Now seem shallow and empty.
My favorite ice cream melts away,
And my stomach has nothing to say.

People talk to me, but I don't hear,
It's like their words don't reach my ear.
I don't want to live like this,
But I don't know how to change this.

I try so hard every single day,
But it seems like I fail in every way.
I cry at night, morning, evening and day,
I just can't seem to keep the tears at bay.

But one day I'm sitting with my family,
They make me laugh and I feel so happy.
In a fraction of a second, I realize,
When was the last time I laughed until my eyes?

I can't remember, it's been so long,
This sadness has held me for so long.
I cry, but for a different reason this time,
I don't want to be in this state of mind.

But I know that things will get better,
That one day, I'll be a go-getter.
I won't cry myself to sleep anymore,
Happiness will come knocking on my door.

And when it does, I'll talk about my pain,
With others who know the struggle and the
strain.
I'll share my story, and give hope and love,
To those struggling, and show them they're
enough.

If today was tough, there's always tomorrow,
Don't give up hope, don't live in sorrow.
If this wasn't the morning where you woke up
feeling great,
Remember, that morning is still yours to make.

This is what a month-old pup has to say

There once was a pup, just one month old,
Who thought he was human, or so he was told.
He lived with his hoomans, who loved him so,
But expressing himself was quite the no-go.

He'd bark and he'd whine, but they didn't
understand,
He wanted food or cuddles, or a playmate at
hand.
But his hoomans just laughed, and scratched his
head,
Not knowing what he wanted, or what he had
said.

He'd watch them eat, with a longing in his eyes,
But when he tried to join in, he was met with
surprise.
"No, no, little one," they would say with a smile,
"You're a pup, not a human, you'll have to wait a
while."

But the pup was determined, to make them see,
That he was just like them, full of love and glee.
He'd wag his tail, and tilt his head,
Hoping his hoomans would understand what he
said.

And then one day, he learned a new trick,
He jumped up and down, with a bark and a lick.
His hoomans were startled, but then they knew,
He wanted to play, and have fun with them too.

From then on, he'd bark and jump and play,
His hoomans understood, and joined in the fray.
And though he was a pup, just one month old,
He was part of the family, a story to be told.

Next time you hear dogs barking at night, know that they are gossiping

As the moon rises up so high,
And stars light up the darkened sky,
Dogs from all around convene,
To gossip, bark, and blow off steam.

They exchange stories from their day,
On how they've chased the cats away,
How they've dug up bones and toys,
And chased birds till they made noise.

They talk about the people too,
Those who pet and feed them too,
They bark at strangers passing by,
With a great ferocity they spy.

And of course, it's all about gossip,
The new strays that they hope would stop,
Fantasies about bones so big,
And what they'll do with 'em when they dig.

Some even talk about next life,
As they imagine a world without strife,
Where bones are plenty, and food is yums,
And they can wag their tails without qualms.

As dawn comes to break the night,
The dogs disperse, with some in sight,
But each one knows he will return,
For more gossip, and tales that burn.

These dogs have a lot to say,
And in their own astute way,
They share their lives, their loves, their joys,
Barking through the night with much noise!

How it fueled me through years, I hope it fuels you too

The way you work is the way you live,
Put in the effort, don't just give.
Focus on doing something great,
With passion and purpose, never too late.

If you don't quit, you're still a winner,
Bravo of your life, never a sinner.
You can do anything you set your mind to,
Be proud of the hard work you do.

Family comes always first,
love and cherish them, for they're your heart's
thirst.
In life, there's nothing as big as being happy,
Finding joy and peace, always snappy.

Stay committed to your dreams and goals,
Never give up, with your heart and soul.
If you take care of things they last,
Endurance and patience come as a blast.

Respect yourself at all times,
Even when others don't, it's not a crime.
Fatt de chakkee, chakk de fatte,
Do your work honestly, without hate.

So stay calm, stay focused,
Achieving what you want, no need to be desperate.
These deep things, worth pondering,
Bring positivity and wisdom, never blundering.

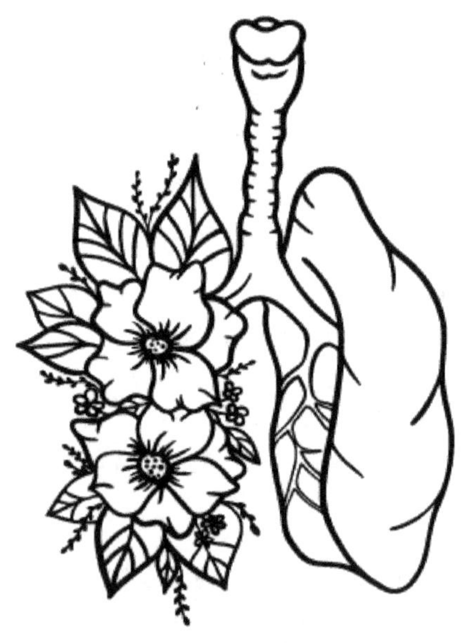

Be the bigger person always

Forgive and move on, always be the bigger
person
It may seem impossible, but it's a valuable
lesson
This process takes time, but it's worth the effort
Acceptance and understanding, the keys to pick
the lock's bolt

It's natural to feel anger and discomfort when
broken
But you have the power to come out of it,
outspoken
Let small disasters protect you from big blunders
Use it as a stepping stone and let it help you
grow fonder

Understand the negative motivation of the
person at hand
Empathize if you can, or mark clear boundaries
to withstand
Don't let emotions dictate how you move
forward
Detach yourself if necessary, and let go of the
cord

There are different ways to forgive, choose your own pace
Breathe a sigh of relief, and let the past be erased
Find spiritual and emotional advancement in your way
Compassion, courage, and fidelity, no matter the fray

So, be the bigger person, and forgive with all your heart
It may be tough, but it's a significant start
Godspeed where necessary, always move on with grace
For giving and growing, in life, is always the best pace

Unusual, it's okay

Unusual, a term so intriguing,
Hard to notice, even harder to bring.
Being unheard, a lesson learned,
Yelling in pain, until it's your turn.

Being heard, like being loved,
But average folks, don't know thereof.
Unusual things wear a peculiar guise,
Difficult to understand, before our eyes.

Hearing someone, means they exist,
A deep form of kindness, we can enlist.
An expression hard to articulate,
But a feeling we cannot negate.

To feel heard, it's profound,
A feeling like never before abound.
Without it, existence feels surreal,
Unusual to the world, so visceral.

Visible on the outside, painful within,
A turmoil we don't know how to begin.
Being heard brings peace and relief,
A chance to unburden, regain our belief.

To wear yellow is beautiful, & to be someone's yellow is more beautiful

To be someone's yellow is to bring joy,
To light up their day and not be coy.
To be the sunbeam that breaks through the clouds,
And lift a heavy heart with the light that surrounds.

It's a feeling of beauty, a soulful delight,
To know that in someone's life, you shine bright.
To bring peace to a troubled mind,
And leave a little love behind.

It's a powerful thing to be someone's spark,
To give them hope when life turns dark.
To lift them up when they feel low,
And let them know they're not alone.

For being someone's yellow is more than just being nice,
It's a true effort to make a difference in another's life.
Imagine if we all made an effort to shine,
What a beautiful world we could leave behind.

So take a moment to be someone's light,
To let them know that everything will be all
right
And watch their spirit soar and fly,
And know that you've been someone's yellow,
and made them sigh.

Next time you see a puppy down the road, this is what he has to say

A lost puppy, small and weak,
Feels so scared, can hardly speak.
Away from mamma, all alone,
Cries in silence, like a mournful tone.

He wants to confide in her,
To feel her warmth, to feel secure.
All he wants is to be with her,
But instead, he's crying in a blur.

The world feels like it's ending now,
As he wanders searching for a new vow.
Hungry and alone, abandoned too,
All he wants is a friend who is true.

People don't treat him very nice,
And his heart breaks like an icy vice.
He thinks that "Dog" spelled backwards is
"God",
But right now, he feels like a fraud.

His little paws leave prints on the ground,
But they go unnoticed, never found.
He's just so sad, wants to go back home,
Wants to stop wandering, stop the roam.

He wants to speak and have someone
understand,
He wants to cry and take someone's hand,
He's been told he's a living being too,
So why won't somebody take him to his mama,
his home, so true?

Heartbroken, he wishes to God above,
To send someone who will hold him with love.
Someone who will feed him like their child,
Cloth him like their own, and forever smile.

Someone who will love him and give him a new
start,
And he will fill all the voids within their heart.
He promises he'll never let his master cry,
He will be there, he will always try.

So, God, please send someone kind and true,
To take him in their arms and love him too.
To tap his forehead with love, hold his paws like
a trophy gold,
To give him the family he's dreamed about; a
new home, a warm fold.

Can't snap out of stress? Just read this

Joy met a foe who thought was a friend,
Known by a name called Stress, penned.

Though Joy was selectively social,
But his wisdom couldn't choose to be anti-social.

They would shilly-shally & mess around
together,
Everyday he comes.

Joy got his intellect weakened,
& thereby his happiness beacon-weakened.

Stress muddled his judgments,
& Joy got a lot cold in life- an ailment.

Zig-zag pattern of wisdom,
Since Stress had his dictum.

Fortunately, Joy's mamma was to his rescue,
Who managed to stop Stress coming by
declaring a curfew.

She sat, heard, & acknowledged Joy,
Who became a pukka Joy.

Joy unfriended Stress,
& felt the ultimate bliss.

Favourite, I'm my favourite

I am my favourite, this is true,
I love myself, through and through,
Not in an egoistic way,
But in a self-love kind of way.
What about you, who do you adore?
Is it yourself, or someone more?

Right from a pollen's brain

A flying pollen in the city,
Drifting on the gentle breeze,
Sights and sounds of life so pretty,
Different perspectives that it sees.

It floats above the bustling streets,
Watching people come and go,
Different colours, varied beats,
Joy, sorrow, yes, even woe.

The buildings rise up to the sky,
Reaching for the clouds so high,
One stands tall, majestic and regal,
While another's dullness is so feeble.

The parks and trees in green surround,
A haven of peace for all around,
Youngsters playing, people strolling,
And lovers hand in hand strolling.

The smell of food, a delightful treat,
Coming from restaurants so discreet,
Bright lights, music, and laughter,
Nature's symphony never after.

The pollen, it sees it all,
Every colour, every hue,
And basks in the endless sprawl,
Of city life, so bright and new.

Different feelings, different vibes,
People lost, others thrive.
Joy and sadness, delight and sorrow,
A blend of emotions that we follow.

So let the pollen keep floating,
Observing and feeling all that's unfolding,
Of this bustling city that we call our own,
For inside, it's where we have grown.

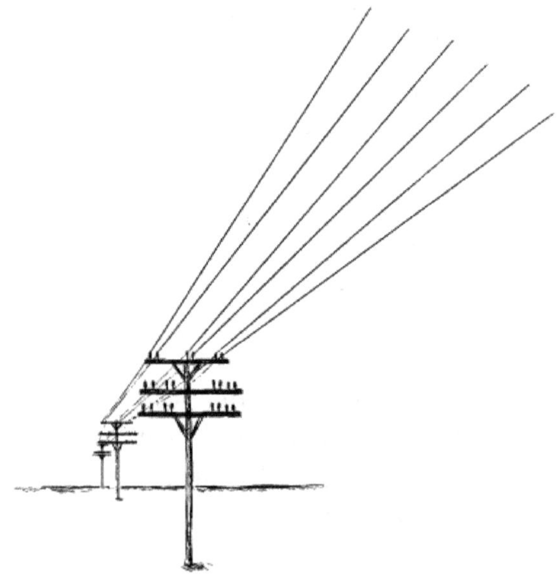

Next time you see the shimmery eyes of a Soldier

On the border I stand so tall,
Far away from my dear shopping mall.
I miss my family, oh so much,
Especially my mom's home-cooked lunch.

But in their letters, they bring me cheer,
Telling me about the pickle they made this year.
And how my sister is growing so fast,
But still a badass, like me in the past.

How I long for Golgappas from my favourite
stall,
But for now, I'll just make do with this wall.
And as I read their words so sweet,
I can almost smell the chapatis' heat.

My father's handwriting, so bold and strong,
Makes me feel like I can go on and on.
And with a piece of maulik wrapped tight,
I know everything will be all right.

So though I'm far away and out of sight,
My love for them will burn ever so bright.
And as I stand vigilant, I'll always remember,
That I'll be back soon, in the loving arms of
September.

Family always comes first

Family always comes first,
A bond that can't be rehearsed,
No matter how far you roam,
Your family always calls you home.

Their love and support are pure,
It's a treasure that will endure,
In good times and in worst,
Family always comes first.

There's always a reason to smile, find it

Once a punctured tyre met Murphy's Law,
Together they joked and laughed with awe
For wherever the tyre tried to go,
Murphy's Law was sure to show.

Flat again? That's no surprise!"
Chuckles Murphy, with twinkling eyes
The tyre groans, " Can't you give me a break?
But Murphy's Law just laughs, for goodness
sake!

The two became fast friends, it's true,
Bound together like glue
Wherever the tyre went, there was Murphy,
Making sure things didn't go too smoothly.

But in the end, the tyre didn't care,
For with Murphy's Law, it learned to share,
The ups and downs, the twists and turns
For the punctured tyre, Murphy's Law always
yearns.

So if you're ever feeling down
With a punctured tyre and a frown,
Remember the friendship of these two,
And find the humor in all that you do!

Why 21?

Twenty-one, a number divine,
On my birthday, it truly shines.
it brings me hope and sight for life,
A magic spell that dissolves strife.
As I hold dear this number so true,
I hope it brings blessings to you too.

www.ingramcontent.com/pod-product-compliance
Lightning Source LLC
LaVergne TN
LVHW010824200726
843508LV00012B/2491